NINETEEN

MAKENZIE CAMPBELL

central
avenue
publishing

2020

To all the places that have held my heart and all
the people who have stood outside the doors with
open arms, ready to hold me.

The poem on page 147 is an homage to Lin Manuel Miranda and his poem written for
and recited at the 2016 Tony Awards.

Published by Central Avenue Publishing, an imprint of Central Avenue Marketing Ltd.
www.centralavenuepublishing.com

NINETEEN

Trade Paperback: 978-1-77168-186-5
Epub: 978-1-77168-187-2
Mobi: 978-1-77168-188-9

Published in Canada
Printed in United States of America

1. POETRY / General   2. POETRY / Women Authors

10 9 8 7 6 5 4 3

THE BEDROOM

The walls are moving closer.

No matter how much I

    scream,

    kick,

    and yell,

no one seems to hear.

Or care?

I am boxed in, holding my hands out, trying

to stop everything from caving in.

But these walls,

they talk,

and they keep whispering,

"There's no room for you here."

Soon enough, I realized I was looking for you in every instance, every song, every sunset, every drop of rain.

When I was with you time slowed down.

It almost stopped.

The world went by in hazy and measured movements.

When you left, all the minutes that were traded for hours
and all the days that turned into years with you
hit me at full force.

Suddenly, the world picked up and ran away without me.

I was not ready.

Time has left me broken.

I know you second-guess yourself. I know you sometimes think you don't mean anything to anybody except your parents (and maybe not even them). I know there are nights where you lie wide awake and contemplate all your imperfections and blemishes.

I know you are insecure and you have this wavering confidence that takes hours to build and only seconds to destroy.

I know that despite all the compliments and words of encouragement and people supporting you, you still have doubts and fears and hesitancies.

I know this.

I know you

because you are me.

I have all these struggles too.

And I'm not here to give you an answer or solution because I do not have one. Not yet. That's something you and I have to discover separately, on our own paths in our different ways.

But I am here to tell you you are not alone. You may feel like it, but I am here, on this earth, feeling these things too.

Let's run through the woods

with the wind on our face

and the soil on our skin

as we escape this sad place.

I see things.

Then I feel things.

And then I write them.

The cycle.

I can hear other planets calling out to me with hollow voices, begging me to make a home of their lonely sands.

I've been damaged

and I use men as a bandage.

But they always fall away

the next morning,

leaving my wound exposed.

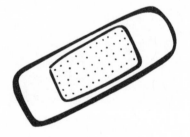

You can feel whole and empty at the same time.

I wonder how many scars I would see

if I cut you open to reveal all your truths.

We collect these small memories

like little pieces of glass

that change color

and reflection

each time we pass them by.

(time and nostalgia both have

a way of coloring a memory

into something grander

than it was)

I'm falling apart slowly

and I hate it.

I hate it.

I want gravity to pull all of me to the ground

instead of me watching pieces of myself float away
one by one.

Every morning I look in the mirror and parts of me are
missing.

Little by little I'm falling apart,

different pieces in different places

each and every day.

I want it over with.

Please someone press fast-forward.

There's nothing worse than watching yourself

unravel in s l o w m o t i o n .

What am I supposed to do with all these broken memories and empty places and painful pictures of us being happy and in love?

There are days

when the sun hides away

and the sky is just a little grey

but I'm not sad

or happy.

I'm just there

feeling empty,

paralyzed in the center of the spectrum.

READ WHEN: you feel heartbroken.

To whoever's heart is hurting, there are three things I want you to know:

1. This pain you are currently feeling, the ache in your chest, the emptiness in your gut, that will last for a while. Days, maybe months. Whoever it is that broke your heart was probably in your life for a long time. Perhaps long enough that you made a home of them. You can't lose your home and be on your feet, smiling, the next day. You can't lose someone that's been in your life for months and be fine the next day. Allow yourself to feel this pain and be okay with its presence for a while.

2. With that being said — the world is not going to end now that they are no longer in yours. There might be a black hole in the spot where they walked out, but these things close up over time and your life will continue on. In most stories I've heard, life actually gets better once the hole closes up and you get to see what a beautiful life you are able to live without an obligation to anyone. Find excitement in your solitude. There may come a day when you never get to live on your own again.

3. Lastly, I love you and I hope you love you. Through all the rainy days I am sure have come and will come again, I hope you are able to see the sunshine that radiates from within you. How your smile glows like the essence of the moon and each time you dance, the stars shine a little brighter. You are beautiful as an individual, and I hope when you look in a mirror that you recognize the thousands of qualities that you carry like the freckles on your cheeks. You are a world of your own and whoever walked away from this world of yours has suffered a great loss. Please do not let their goodbye make you believe anything less.

Do you feel it all fading away?

Can you feel every conversation slowly slipping out of your head? Each laugh forgotten, every encounter falling away? The people you have built your life with are about to be ripped from their foundation and you must build new walls with new faces.

While both exciting and scary, the goodbye will be the hardest you have ever known.

(homage to the transitioning, the moving, the traveling,
the ones constantly saying goodbye to say
hello to new lands)

I am sorry I have hurt you.

I did not mean to.

But my intentions do not matter.

Because you are spilling over like the dirty rainwater in full gutters.

And I can feel the aching in your bones

because of me.

I do not know how to make it better.

Every time I try to speak I can see how each word is like a dagger.

There are no words or explanations for why I must leave you.

It is only that my heart is telling me to go.

And I must follow where it leads me

even if that means leaving you

behind.

I am just going through the motions

like a fish in the ocean

who keeps

      swimming

      swimming

      swimming

to survive.

Not really leading (or living)

any type of life.

I search

    in words

    in sunsets

    in rain

    in the changing of the weather

for explanations

    as to why I feel

    so empty and alone

    and why I still

    long for you.

Isn't it ironic that some of our best, most treasured memories are of people whose eyes are no longer familiar and shadows are too distant to make out who they are anymore.

Have you ever found yourself in a room full of people, one where everyone seems to be shouting conversations except you, and you have somehow wound up leaning against the wall in a corner, staring at your shoes, thinking you would rather be anywhere but here in this room, and never felt more lonely in your entire life?

The walls turned to water.

The carpet to seaweed.

The room was an ocean

in which she found herself

suspended

and thinking

she could lie still

and watch the fishes swim around her bare feet

and slowly let herself

     slip away.

I hope she chose to save herself.

Every time,

     I hope.

I am a kite

    that is running

        out of wind

            to carry me

    and

                keep me

                    afloat.

I thought of Rome.

Of the Colosseum and Palatine Hill crumbling away little by little each day.

Even with all these cracks and scars and crumbling walls, fragmented ceilings and danger warnings, people still travel from around the world to visit each place. Thousands take pictures to capture its beauty and always have a little piece to look back on. Some just stand in awe, jaw dropped, at the strength of these walls and the age of these stairs. And even though everything is falling apart, their beauty glows in the sunlight.

And then I thought of you.

You, with cracks and scars and a collapsing heart and crumbling spirit.

You, who may right now be falling apart.

You, who is absolutely beautiful with all of these attributes.

You, whose beauty and grace I would travel across the world to witness.

When you are wide awake at three in the morning crying, screaming, fuming, or silently hurting . . .

write to me.

Sometimes black holes exist on earth.

Sometimes they appear, all of a sudden, in your life

     and maybe you lose a few friends;

     maybe it sucks away your job

     or swallows up a lover who you

     thought would be around forever.

With all this darkness surrounding you, you might even lose yourself.

It's difficult to see the bright side when the central void is pitch black and all your little stars seem to keep blinking out one by one.

But sooner or later that black hole will collapse on itself and you'll be hit with the warmth of the sun. At night the moon will shine and little by little the stars will begin to glow and though your life has fallen apart, you will slowly rebuild yourself (perhaps a life even better than before) below a new horizon.

Be patient,

     and believe in these words.

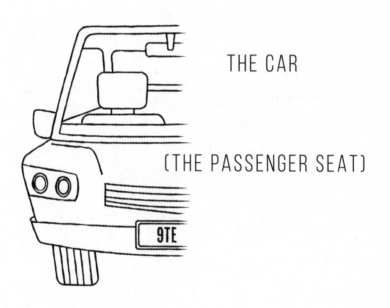

THE CAR

(THE PASSENGER SEAT)

Someone else is driving.

I'm not in control.

I can scream and shout directions

but it's up to you to choose

whether you turn right or left,

whether you stop or go.

I can scream and shout I love you

but it's up to you to choose

if I'm someone you'll pursue.

If I'm someone you could love.

Pluto fell in love with the sun, but the sun was in love with the moon.

Pluto would try to inch closer only to realize he was stuck in the same circular orbit of watching and waiting and unrequited love...

until eventually not only did the sun and the stars discount his existence

but the astronauts and scientists too.

I've been trying to tell you that the wind seems to blow in the opposite direction.

So every time I try to call out to you, my words are carried away before ever reaching your location.

The most tragic love story of all was the one written in their hearts, but never typed out on paper.

(you could both love each

other and neither would know,

if you don't tell each other so.)

He collects hearts

and leaves a trail

of empty souls

(and blank faces)

in his

wake.

I should have never made a home of you.

People are not homes.

Not when they can stand up and walk away whenever they decide it is time to go.

You became bored with the things you once adored.

That's why I'm so scared every time a man says he loves the way I push my hair behind my ears, and my spontaneous giggle.

Because you used to love all these things.

Until you didn't.

I have wasted too many years picking daisies,
plucking the "He loves me" and "He loves me not"
from them.

But I know the second he reappears in my life I'll waste
too many more.

You fool me each and every time into thinking you care.

That maybe this time we could be the perfect pair.

But then you open my message and don't reply and leave me just wondering why...

I'm undeserving of love.

And then "At Last" plays on the turntable, and at last I don't feel alone anymore as I drape my arms over your ghost and dance the night away, pretending I can still feel your heartbeat drumming against your chest, that I can still taste the colors of your soul.

But the song is only a few minutes long and there are no more grooves in the track. I'm left standing in an empty room with a broken heart that still loves you and is whispering,

"Come back."

Do you remember our hearts pounding, screaming,

"THIS IS IT!"

This is the one who is supposed to be holding you right now. This very moment is right. We are right. We are good together.

Every skin cell vibrated when you held me. Do you remember that?

Do you recall these moments?

Or are they just misplaced recollections that only I seem to have?

It is pathetic

how I cry

over you when

you aren't even

mine,

but I can't help

that you draw me back

like the shore draws back the tide.

There's an eviction notice on the front lawn. I've stayed too long. Hung on to these walls like old paint, clinging to the (few) good memories and ignoring the empty promises, all the times you've been dishonest.

At least something gave me notice that I must leave, even if it breaks a part of me.

I want love so bad.

That's why on my lonely nights

I run back to our memories

and fall a little in love

with the nostalgia and idea of you.

I can't get "over" you

if I don't have anyone else

to give my love to.

I am not strong enough to carry

all of what I feel

alone.

I'm scared I'll never get over you.

And that every time I meet a man

I'll think of you, and how he lacks

what you had.

So I'll search and search and go through men just like I go
through books or hair ties, only to be 28 and realize

that I'm still searching for you in the eyes of every
stranger.

It is a beautiful thing to be able to see the goodness in someone when nobody else does.

But you have to know when to let go.

I sat down in the same spot where you kissed her and asked myself: why was she better than me?

Why was she the one you kissed?

She doesn't even love you.

She wanted someone just for the night.

And you offered yourself up so easily,

while I've been here begging for a lifetime.

I don't know how to be as beautiful as she was in your eyes. I don't know how to make you laugh the same way or tell the same jokes. I don't take my coffee the way she did or wear the same clothes. I don't know how to be her.

Please stop trying to make me the ghost of your past lover.

I've written about you

    and written about you

       and written about you

with hundreds of words,

gallons of ink,

and thousands of sleepless nights.

I have made you immortal between these lines.

What if we aren't the person

made for the person

made for us?

I've made a home of all different materials—

the sands at the beach, the window seat of my favorite coffee shop, the swing at a childhood park—

but I am proud to say that your arms are no longer one of them.

We sit in silence. The thick kind of silence that imprisons words and feelings in your throat. If they do find the strength to make it to your lips they never get past that point. Never release into the air. Just freeze there like icicles that eventually burn your skin.

Neither of us dares to speak. This is us digging the grave of us. Every word unsaid is another foot of soil removed. We are slowly falling towards the center of the earth. Our hands are filthy with secrets and mistakes we dare not tell.

I lift my chin, slowly, then my eyes, and turn towards you. I've come to know every part of you—except this look. The amber of your eyes has faded. Your skin is worn. I think this is defeat.

We never once break eye contact. I can see you searching me for a glimmer, some sort of sign, to pack the soil back in and try again. But you see that same look pasted to my face as well.

It is over and we both know this truth.

I take a deep breath as you gently nod, signifying this is goodbye, and we both begin to climb into the grave. I lower myself and rest my head on the cold earth, staring up at the grey sky. My hands are crossed against my chest, the deal is done, we tried our best. But I've come to learn that sometimes trying your best just isn't enough. Not in love. Not when the universe doesn't permit it.

I wonder if you will cry? If flowers will one day bloom above our heads and if you will be the one to water them? Or will I?

I hope beautiful things one day come from this goodbye. It means we did something right and it was worth it in some twisted and abstract way. With all these wrongs branded upon our hearts, I only hope we can do one thing right.

I hope this dead romance will feed the birds so they can sing to all the hopeful young lovers in the park, as they once did to us.

We both believed in love.

But one of us believed in it more than the other.

I am learning to accept the fact that you will always be in my heart. Your name has made a home of it even though your body said differently as I watched you walk out of my life.

For a long time I thought I just needed time.

Time.

Time to forget about the kisses and the heat of your hand in mine. The three a.m. phone calls and fits of laughter born deep in my belly.

But time can't erase memories so timeless.

So,

I am learning to live with this small piece of me that will always love you, hopelessly,

and am moving on as best I can.

I hope you write about me sometimes.

Even if it's only on a crumpled napkin or hidden away in a secret journal, or words inside a letter you will never send.

Still, I hope you do.

There are loves in your life that you will never get over.

Your heart will never heal or recover.

And all you can do is learn to live with that.

THE SHOWER

I'll let the shower run

and feel the drops of water

slip through my fingers

just like you did

over and over and over again.

Be careful.

He is magic.

And as you should know, all magic is deception.

Do

not

trust

him.

Not

again.

He keeps promising he's coming

back home.

But his heart is on

vacation.

So even when he's here, he's not really

here.

And the space between these four walls is

vacant.

I can't believe I confused your

selfishness for selflessness

and pitied the victimization of yourself

when it was I who was truly the victim.

Soon enough you'll be thirty and wondering how the hell you got from here to there. You'll look back at old pictures and swear that was just yesterday and then realize that yesterday was ten years ago.

And your heart will both rise and fall at the thought of those Friday night parties you used to get too drunk at, the times you screamed *High School Musical* songs at the top of your lungs while riding shotgun in your friend's car with the windows down on the highway.

You'll think of the time you and Jordan danced alone in her bedroom to some throwback R&B or the time you and Hailey and Abi laughed until you cried while sitting "criss-cross applesauce" on her white carpets at four in the morning.

You'll think of all the boys you carelessly kissed and all the late nights spent sitting by a fire playing Never Have I Ever and Truth or Dare.

And then reality will drag you back and demand you pay the bills, do the laundry, wash the dog. Pick up the kids from school, cook dinner, and somehow find enough time to hold your husband before you fall into bed.

And though you love this busy life and beautiful family you've built for yourself, there will always be a piece of you that misses being nineteen and young with no responsibilities and the entire world at your fingertips.

People will use

  "I love you"

as a currency

to take advantage of you.

He carved me out like a pumpkin.

Made me spill all my

thoughts,

secrets,

dreams,

until he knew everything.

Then October passed us

quietly

and he left me on his doorstep

to rot.

WHY WON'T YOU LEAVE

ME AND

MY HEART ALONE?

go find someone else

to hold

(back)

"I loved him and it broke me,"

                I confessed.

She rolled her eyes and said,
"You are too young to know what love is.
Don't throw that word around so meaninglessly,
and stop being so dramatic."

So I stopped, never talked about it again,
silently went to sleep,

        and cried about it in my dreams.

I let them in to let me feel something again.

It's been too long without a feeling.

Forever, actually.

I'll sip what you give me so I no longer feel empty.

Every kiss I give is in turn a kiss to myself to heal my bruising.

Is this me losing?

Everything?

Myself?

Who am I anymore?

Do you like living a lie?

Wearing a mask all the time?

Doesn't your face need air?

Let your skin breathe

and your cheeks feel the

droplets of rain pool in your pores.

Your skin is too clean.

That isn't beauty,

to hide all your imperfections,

to hide you—

it's a tragedy.

One full of pretending with

a round-the-clock smile.

Don't you want a happy ending?

You won't find it like this.

The saddest thing

       is to see a dream

       crumple and disintegrate

       away.

When you were so close

       to getting to know her

       all you had to do

       was round the corner,

       but you sat in the

       middle of the road

       and claimed you were too tired

       and wasted it away.

Each letter undresses me.

Every sentence opens me up

and takes a piece of my heart

and mind and puts them

on the page.

This is my undoing.

Here I lie naked between these lines.

I am completely vulnerable.

You've got those ocean eyes.

The kind where every blink pulls me in with the tide.

I can forget a face but I can't forget a name.

Letters (in that specific order) seem to have a way of sticking to my tongue and rolling off of it quite easily, sometimes unknowingly, on my lonely nights.

God give me strength to look past his deceptive eyes
and move on.

I shove my toes into the dirt and
immediately come to a stop.
I will not run behind you anymore,
chasing your love like a dog.
I am learning my self-worth
and how to demand it.

Once you've burned all these pictures and memories
you cannot collect the ashes.

You cannot keep them in your little yellow tin and place
them on your shelf.

That is not letting go.

That is not freedom.

You must let the ashes of the past be carried away by the
wind after you watch the fire die.

And then you must turn around and walk away with
grace.

My lips are in a pretty package on your doorstep.

I cut them off and sent them to you.

They were stained with your taste

and I felt it was only right to give that back,

along with the jeans and movies you left behind.

I stood in front of the mirror for hours,

mastering the art of smiling

and pretending

that I was not broken

and you were not the reason why.

I may not have been able to keep my heart, but I've kept my strength.

You do not have

the authority

to hurt me

anymore.

THE PARK

I'm sitting on the left swing, pumping my legs, and feeling the wind push against my shoulders as I climb higher and higher.

The right swing sits still without you.

Do you remember how we used to sit here and talk for hours? How the sun kissed us goodbye and the stars started to peek out of hiding? All the late nights that I snuck away to be with you? I couldn't resist the way the moonlight pooled in your hair. I couldn't resist you.

I miss the days both swings swung.

And both of us were happy

as love lifted us higher.

In the war of love,

the battle between
emotion and logic
is the most brutal.

He said,

"Why are you so afraid of love?"

I replied,

"I'm not.

I am afraid of mistaking what we have for love

and this confusion leaving me broken

like it has so many times before."

There are many things I would like to tell you

but I've never known how to be brave like that.

A little boat

in a glass bottle

floating aimlessly at sea

the water kisses its walls

while willing it to sail free

but even after all the kisses

and the endless nights spent near

the boat will never touch the water

leaving what's left of this love unclear.

(we love each other but we cannot be

together—what a confusing truth of ours)

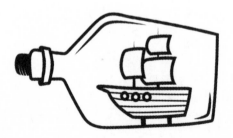

I don't want to be your
late night
last minute
"hey let's hook up" call.

But I don't want to say no
and lose the opportunity for you to hold me.

Nothing feels better than being in your arms.

Is it wrong I let you leave me
but run back when you say you want me
for one night?

It's definitely not dignified.

But I am selfish and self-destructing
and let you take advantage of me
all in the name of
love.

Did you say

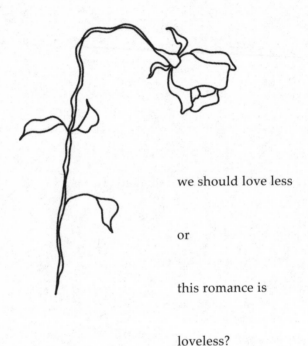

we should love less

or

this romance is

loveless?

There should be a name for the eternal inbetweenness of friendship and lovers.

The nature of you and me.

Are there doors in your mind? Some closed and locked
with secrets to hide? Some wide open like a book—
begging to be held by anyone's hands? Does your head
sometimes feel on fire? With all those memories that burn
(the good and the bad)? Nostalgia can do that to you.
Heartbreak too. Do you sometimes wish you could be
someone new? And dump all the keys to all your doors
somewhere where nobody has been before? And nobody
could find them? Then maybe you wouldn't feel so lost.
But you can't just put your life on pause. It doesn't work
that way. You just have to trudge on day by day and
pretend you know which direction your feet are taking
you and where your mind is at.

Hiding everything you ever feel behind a smile is protecting everyone else but weighing your own soul down.

Do you know how much pain your soul can carry?

How long before your rib cage breaks and folds you in half?

Letting your scars show is not a weakness. Talking about the things that have caused you to ache is not a shortcoming.

It is strength.

It is courage.

It is self-care.

(It is necessary.)

We search for truth in a world full of lies. We want honesty but are conditioned to be its counter.

Our tongues perpetrate false statements faster than our minds can think of their implications. Our mouths form dishonest stories more often than our eyes tell the truth.

We condemn each other and ourselves to a world of falsities then blame everyone else for living in it.

There are two sides to every story.

Do not fall into the trap of believing in the one told more often or more loudly

without ever seeking the other's truth.

Sometimes it's not their fault.

Sometimes it's yours.

Do not make blame a habit.

It is selfish to balance 2 people,

2 kisses,

2 no commitments,

when each person on the scale is reaching for the heart at the center, blind to their weight and their counterweight and your games of symmetry and charm.

You are so scared that you are going to get hurt that you hurt the other person first, but if you love like this you will, in the end, only ever be hurting yourself.

Don't blame the scars of those who left on the ones trying to stay and heal.

Stop watering dead relationships and expecting them

to grow.

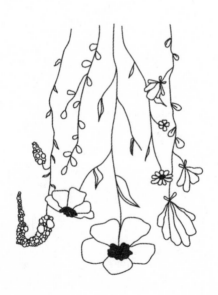

Pride silences me.

I've come to know the damage that can be done when I don't listen to her. The embarrassment, the inferiority.

But the love I hold for you burns within me, its flames growing wilder. How do I silence a booming fire without reducing myself to cinders?

Do you follow your head or your heart

when both are equally right and equally wrong?

My mind likes to travel to different planets.

It's a bad habit.

When my problems pollute the oceans and the trees

      I leave

for red dust storms and the comfort of craters.

The universe is my home,

and Earth is a stranger.

We crave to feel a vulnerable and empathetic connection with another soul, yet the fear of taking off our masks and revealing our true features prevents us from satisfying that desire.

When you've arrived at that dreadful place—

the place where all your negative thoughts collect—

think of me and how proud I am of you just the way you are.

When your mind begins to turn the idea of leaving over and over in your head,

think of me and how I believe you have a purpose.

When you sit on the edge of your bathtub crying while holding that blade in your shaking hand,

think of me and how I know better things are yet to come—if only you put down your weapon.

When your toes are dangling off the edge of that bridge and the winds seem to whisper through your hair, "Let go,"

think of me and how I begged you to stay.

Sometimes there are no words to describe how I feel.

These thoughts are caged birds inside of me, violently trying to escape.

Their wings pound against my ribs, shoving air in every direction but through my lips, letting out distress calls, shrieks, only I can hear. I wish I knew how to let them out. I wish I could let them fly.

Set them free.

But they never seem to find their way.

There is this double standard

where a boy's loss of virginity calls for a celebration

but a girl's calls for derision and exclusion.

The same act leads to congratulations and
disappointment.

He did not inspire any words inside me.

For him, I could not write any poetry.

And that is how I knew

he was not

the one.

I never felt a spark. Not even the distant heat of one.

I want to be set on fire.

I want to love so fiercely that the tips of my fingers become flames that can be seen for hundreds of miles.

I want to burn everything around us to ash, so that we are all that exist in this space.

> You and me.

> And these embers.

Everyone will know how deeply we have fallen into love.

Or rather, how we've crashed into it, igniting these flames in the first place.

He is sweet

and kind

and everything

I have ever wanted

which is why

I cannot figure out

why I do not

want him.

(love never runs the way you wish it to)

I am trying to find a way to describe this sinking feeling in my chest.

The feeling that knows the end is coming and that I will be the one to tell him.

To have so much and complain about having so little

      reveals your selfish nature and childish privilege.

For all your gifts you see wrapped in plainness,

      which to others are lavishly wrapped in gold.

Do we put up these walls

and dig these trenches

to keep other people out?

Or to keep ourselves in?

Now I want you

   when you used to want me.

We've always had an issue

   with bad timing.

We have belittled ourselves
into accepting the standards
set by paper magazines and
digital corrections.
We strive for it all our lives
when we know
the shape of her legs
isn't real
and his hair
doesn't shine like that,
but they tell us
this is what's beautiful
and we live our whole lives
thinking we are not.

I am constantly falling out of love

and back into it.

When did others' perception of you become more important than your own opinion?

your heart is a rock that can withstand

windstorms

snowstorms

earthquakes

&

hurricanes

if only you believe in it

(and repeat this to yourself.)

Don't get it twisted.

My life isn't poetic.

It's a mess.

But there are places

where flowers happen

to grow from the compost.

There are wars waged between our hearts and our heads
and somehow we manage to stay on our feet.

That is strength.

In its strongest form.

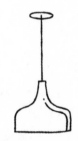

THE COFFEE SHOP

He is my cup of coffee every morning.

A moment with him is equivalent to a triple shot.

I shouldn't dare say what a kiss can do to me.

His lips touched mine

and suddenly

all the colors in the world

hit me at full force.

Writing poetry is trying to find
the right words to describe
how his hair falls around his
face at two in the morning
when he whispers secrets
in the dark.

I am enamored

    by the complexity

        of your personality.

Have you ever had this:

Where you are pulled to someone's chest as they wrap their arms around you

and then your entire body is pressed against theirs

> hands on back
>
> stomach on stomach
>
> cheek on chest.

And even though you are as close as physically possible

you can feel their arms tighten around you even more, as if being physically close was not enough.

As if they wanted to pull you so close that your souls intertwined.

And you close your eyes and hold on tight for the ride.

Because this, the closeness, the intimacy, is something you've been waiting for

all.

your.

life.

I will make a constellation

out of words

and name it after you.

Kiss me slow

      and soft

to draw out all the poison

others have placed in my heart.

You always saw me for what I could be
and I never saw that in myself.

(a thank-you)

We are young

and in love

and stumbling

all over each other's

hearts

leaving marks

that will

definitely sting

later on.

Your smile is a

delicacy.

My fingers trace the surface of your skin.

I swear I can see sparks fly.

A blue electromagnetic pulse that beats quicker the closer you and I get.

You have this pull over my heart.

Every time you look at me, speak to me, so much as breathe in my direction,

my heart gravitates towards yours like a magnet.

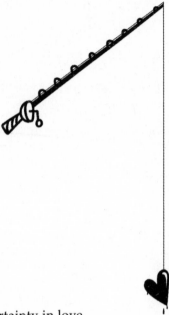

You don't get certainty in love.

That's not how it works.

You get to throw your heart out on a line and hope you catch someone.

Tell me,

is it better to be with somebody who is a risk but you love completely

or to be with a person who is safe and certain

and just settle?

Relationships are hard work.

But so are gardens.

You can't seriously expect to keep your hands clean and still watch beautiful things grow?

I looked at him with sad eyes

and said,

"I just don't think our love is written in the stars."

He looked at me, ready to challenge.

"I will

      write our love in the stars,

            carve our love into the moon,

                  scar our love on the sun.

"I will travel hundreds of thousands of miles.

      Light years, even.

"And if that's not enough,

      I'll visit every universe and

            etch our love into reality there."

You have awoken my heart. I'm not sure how, or why, but I'm lying here, your scent still lingering in my clothes, and smiling at the thought of your fingertips grazing my elbow.

It's five in the morning and I'm running my fingers
through your hair

thinking,

"If this is how I woke up every morning

I could live with that."

Each new piece of information

>his coffee order

>his favorite color

>his father's name

>his love for his mother

is a new dot on my paper.

Since the moment we met, I've slowly been connecting them. Trying to make up who he is, who he has been, perhaps who he will be.

He is a constellation, unfinished, that I have miles left to discover.

It's difficult to capture the essence of you within these words.

There are flowers that grow inside her chest.

They are not seasonal.

They are always growing.

And every time she smiles, I swear a new seed sprouts.

Her simple presence moves mountains
and paints sunsets.

To me,

poetry is a sort of therapy.

One that never asks or intrudes, but waits

patiently on the corner of my desk until I run to

it for aid and spill my ink over blank pages.

And it listens, without judgement, to every

breaking bone and throbbing scar and slowly, one

by one, the words begin to stitch my wound

closed.

Soon there will be no mark at all.

At least for now, while these pages are open and

bleeding.

love is love is love is love is love is love is love is love is
love is love is love is love is love is love is love is love is
love is love is love is love is love is love is love is love is
love is love is love is love is love is love is love is love is
love is love is love is love is love is love is love is love is
love is love is love is love is love is love is love is love is
love is love is love is love is love is love is love is love is
love is love is love is love is love is love is love is love is
love is love is love is love is love is love is love is love is
love is love is love is love is love is love is love is love is
love is love is love is love is love is love is love is love is
love is love is love is love is love is love is love is love is
love is love is love is love is love is love is love is love is
love is love is love is love is love is love is love is love is
love is love is love is love is love is love is love is love is
love is love is love is love is love is love is love is love is
love is love is love is love is love is love is love is love is
love is love is love is love is love is love is love is love is
love is love is love is love is love is love is love is love is
love is love is love is love is love is love is love is love is
love is love is love is love is love is love is love is love is
love is love is love is love is love is love is **love is love**.

(Until all the hate and bias and judgement is gone, this
cannot be repeated enough.)

He is the breath of fresh air that reminds me of what I deserve and how you were not that.

You are teaching me

how to let myself

be loved.

you make me want to

write love songs

and pretty poems

and paint sunsets with words

He took my hand and spun me
around in the center of
the room without any music
playing, with all the
people watching, and that's
when I knew I wanted to
dance with him for the rest
of my forever.

He introduced me to colors I didn't even know existed.

He told me the day he met me,

"The entire universe revolves around us. This whole thing was made for us. The meteorites, the asteroids, the shooting and falling stars, the Big Bang, the rivers, the oceans, the one land being split apart over thousands of years into seven, the first creatures, the dinosaurs, natural selection, evolution, extinction, the first humans, the cavemen, the writings on the walls, hieroglyphics, the pyramids, the Roman Empire, new generations, my parents meeting and falling in love, your parents meeting and falling in love, you being born in October, me being born in September, us growing up without the slightest clue each other existed, and then meeting today.

"The whole thing starts when the universe starts. We were meant to meet. From the start of time this was our fate. The universe was put together solely so this could happen. This. Us. We are meant to be. The universe tells me so."

THE CAR

- THE DRIVER'S SEAT -

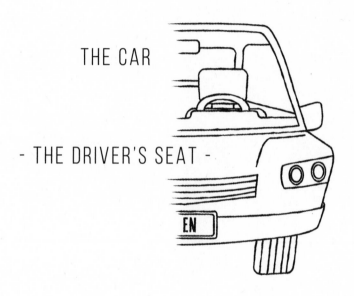

You can't be in pursuit of the destination.

You have to be in pursuit of the journey.

It's all about how you get there.

What you learn on the way.

To leave everything I know

in search of the magic I need

to fill the empty parts of my soul

is a risk I am willing to take.

There are still mountains to climb and oceans to cross,

but I am happy with how far I've come

and the trail I've left

behind me.

Those who are able to find true happiness find it not in the material but in the simple smell of cinnamon, the eyes of a friend, and the sunrise of a new day.

Your words traveled through my ears and

wrapped around my soul

then carried the weight of each insecurity out of my
body and let them float far away.

focus

on the

OPPORTUNITIES

not the

OBSTACLES

and see how your

mindset

CHANGES.

The answers you are looking for are within yourself—

run to a mirror, child, and get lost in it.

I have found comfort

in the flowers

and the muted colors

their petals cast

on my face

in the sunlight.

You never think that your dreams will come true and then one day, after hundreds of tedious, repetitive weeks of hard work and dedication, you open your eyes and there you are with your dream in your hand, slowly becoming your reality.

I am excited for the future

and the colors

and the experiences

and the confetti.

And sometimes things don't go as planned. And maybe that's a good thing, because too often we chase these moments around only to find out they are the wrong ones and the right ones have been patiently waiting in front of us all along.

we grow

we love

we become heartbroken

we pick ourselves up

we learn to love again

All things that fall apart can be brought back together.

Do not lose hope when you see your life in shambles.

You can bring it back together.

Carry on, my darling.

The flower may get knocked down by the wind,

but that is the only way her seeds can be carried

and spread to bloom beautifully around the world.

Instead,

I am the world's canvas
and each new location
colors me.

Every city I discover,
every treasure I uncover,
every friend and every lover,
paints me blues and
reds and yellows.

I hope by the end
I am drenched in
experience and color.

I am just trying to figure this all out.

What I'm supposed to be doing

and where I'm supposed to be.

Who I'm meant to fall for,

who will break my heart,

whose heart I will break.

I'm walking down this path

with absolutely no idea

what I'm doing...

But the important thing is:

I'm doing it.

I did not like where my road was leading.

It wasn't mine.

It had been paved by others before I even had a name.

My destiny had been decided before I was able to speak.

And for the past nineteen years I've kept my head up and toes pointed forward, carefully placing one foot in front of the other.

But I am sick of following the grey concrete that others chose.

Today, I have set out to pave my own path.

Today, I choose to change my destiny and live life by my own rules.

I hope you find this courage too.

If I had never met you,

I never would have gotten here.

So you broke me, in the worst way,

but this pain bloomed into a blessing

and took me down a beautiful path

that I get to live each and every day.

I think

      there is a piece of me

      buried on each continent.

I must

      follow the call of the winds

      and in my adventures

      find my completion.

Darling, you need sleep.

All your worries

fears

anxieties

can wait.

You need to learn how to take care of yourself.

This is step #1.

Do not let these worries leak into your dreams and control you.

Instead, close your eyes and travel far away for a few hours.

Half the battle is choosing

to continue walking

down life's path

and ignoring the

aches of your feet.

This little bump in the road makes for a good story,
but it is not the end of the story.

I am not bound to these domestic soils and street signs.

I cannot be.

My feet ache for travel.

They long to walk across the cobblestone streets of Dubrovnik and hike along the ocean trails of Cinque Terre and at the end of the day be swollen from experience and priceless memories.

There are lives being lived

and footprints being left

in all walks of the world.

Do not be afraid if you are

the first print on an

unbeaten path.

You are guiding those lost

behind you to the light

and you are guiding

yourself to success.

You are right where you are meant to be.

You have a story worth telling.

Why don't you stay awhile and entertain us?

All I want is for you to love me for me and I will love you for you and all our flaws will be small in each other's eyes because there will be too much love to ever make us question our happiness together.

How do I explain

this little ball of light
circulating in the center
of my soul
and
cascading out of my pores?

It is happiness, in its purest form.

It must be.

It's like life has kissed
the tip of my nose
and blessed my
heart with
goodness and
happy thoughts.

I hope

you allow yourself

to be a river

                    fluid and ever-moving

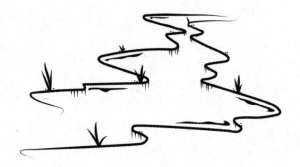

This is the end.

I hope you look back at me and smile.

And then look forward towards the sun at your new beginning.

Special thanks to all the hearts that helped me create:

James DeBono for your constant support and guidance.

Michelle Halket for bringing my ideas to life and finding homes for them to rest.

Courtney Peppernell for always supporting me.

Hannah Juth for the wonderful illustrations.

Lindsay for the beautiful cover and guidance.

Family & friends for giving me the tools to be who I am today and embracing all parts of me.

Readers I am lucky enough to have for reading my little books and making dreams come true.

Makenzie Campbell grew up in the Pacific Northwest and has been expressing herself through poetry since grade school. Following the success of her debut, *2am Thoughts*, Makenzie continues her writing journey with her new collection, *Nineteen*, inspired by her experience transitioning into adulthood. Makenzie is pursuing a degree in psychology at Washington State University, and her little free time is spent traveling the world and exploring the wild trails of the Cascades.

@makenzie.campbell.poetry